How Odd

by J. C. Cunningham
illustrations by Abby Carter

Harcourt Brace & Company

Orlando Atlanta Austin Boston San Francisco Chicago Dallas New York Toronto London

"Deb!" said Mom. "Your room is a mess! Get a mop! Get a box! Get to work!"

"Well," said Deb with a nod, "Mom is right." Deb got to work on the mess.

"How odd," said Deb. "Bess
Hen and Tom Fox. How did
they get here?"

4

"How odd," said Deb. "My bell, set of ten pens, and red top. How did they get here?"

"How odd," said Deb. "My doll Meg and Meg's leg. How did they get here? I bet Meg fell."

6

"How odd," said Deb. "My rock set, box of logs, hot rocket, and pom-poms. How did they get here? I can't tell."

"How odd," said Deb. "My dotted socks, net, wishing well, and jet. How did they get here? Yes, this IS odd."

8

"Well, Mom," said Deb, "it was a lot of work, but no more mess!"

"Good job, Deb!" said Mom with a nod. "Where did you put everything?"

"In my closet!" said Deb.
Out popped Bess Hen, Tom
Fox, the bell, the set of ten
pens, the red top, Meg and
Meg's leg. . .

the rock set, the box of logs,
the hot rocket, the pom-poms,
the dotted socks, the net, the
wishing well, and the jet!

"How odd," said Deb.